"WHY AM I GOING TO THE HOSPITAL?"

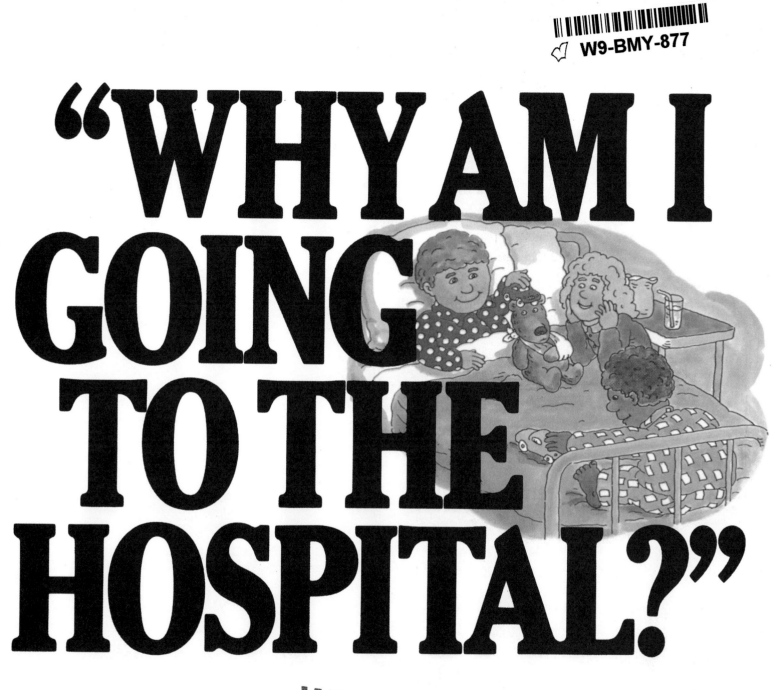

Written by Claire Ciliotta and Carole Livingston.
Illustrated by Dick Wilson. Designed by Paul Walter.

First Carol Publishing Group Edition 1992

A Lyle Stuart Book
Published by Carol Publishing Group
Lyle Stuart is a registered trademark of Carol Communications, Inc.

Editorial Offices : 600 Madison Avenue, New York, NY 10022
Sales & Distribution Offices: 120 Enterprise Avenue, Secaucus, NJ 07094
In Canada: Canadian Manda Group, P.O. Box 920, Station U, Toronto,
Ontario, M8Z 5P9, Canada

Queries regarding rights and permissions should be addressed to Carol
Publishing Group, 600 Madison Avenue, New York, NY 10022

Manufactured in the United States of America
ISBN 0-8184-0568-6

Typesetting by Ella-Type, Hollywood, California
Mechanicals by Louellen and Lisa

Carol Publishing Group books are available at special discounts
for bulk purchases, for sales promotions, fund raising, or
educational purposes. Special editions can also be created to
specifications. For details contact: Special Sales Department,
Carol Publishing Group, 120 Enterprise Ave., Secaucus, NJ 07094

10 9 8 7 6 5 4 3 2 1

Library of Congress Cataloging-in-Publication Data

Ciliotta, Claire.
   Why am I going to the hospital?

   Summary: Explains some of the things that happen in
a hospital and some of the things one can see--all
designed to give "star" treatment to people who need to
be made well.
   1. Hospitals--Juvenile literature. 2. Children--
Preparation for medical care--Juvenile literature.
[1. Hospitals] I. Livingston, Carole. II. Wilson,
Dick, 1930-   ill.   III. Title.
RA963.5.C54   362.1'1   81-16642
                        AACR2

Why Am I Going to the Hospital?

This book is for you – and for kids like you – who sometimes have to go to the hospital. So this book is about hospitals too.

First, let's agree on one thing: Nobody likes to go to a hospital – not even a grownup. Except maybe a mother who is going to have a baby.

But going to a hospital sometimes is necessary. So let's find out how you happened to go to a hospital in the first place.

There are lots of different ways.

Maybe you got sick. (That happens to everyone once in a while.) Now, most of the time when you become sick your folks take care of you. If you're only a little sick it almost seems like fun. You get hot soups and cold fruit juices and coloring books and sometimes a special toy to play with.

Other times, when your folks can't help you to get well they may take you to a doctor. The doctor may examine you and give you medicine to take until you feel better.

But there are times when the job of making you well is too big for just a little medicine and a lot of loving family care. It's so big that the doctor decides you need special "star" treatment. That's when you go to a hospital.

You probably have seen hospitals on television. You might have a friend who was in the hospital or your Grandma may have been ill and spent some time in one. (On TV you sometimes see people lying in beds with doctors and nurses running all over the place. Very exciting.)

Actually, there's lots more to a hospital than just doctors and nurses.

Sometimes, a hospital is the place to go when you need certain tests. No, not the kind you have in school – these are tests for your body that need special machines. Only the hospitals have the people who know how to work these machines – because they've been specially trained.

When people go to have these tests they usually don't stay at the hospital. They go home right after the tests. Other times people go to hospitals if they need to have x-rays taken. (These are pictures of what's inside you.) You don't have to stay in the hospital to have x-rays taken either.

But most of all, a hospital, and all the people who work there, have one goal: that is to help you, the patient, get well.

A hospital is like a factory with all sorts of people on the staff, each having a special job to do.

Let's talk about the people who work in a hospital.

There are lots of nurses, usually dressed in white. They even wear white shoes! The nurses are very important because they'll be spending more time with you than anyone else.

In fact, they are so important that they have enough nurses so that there will be someone to take care of you around the clock – all twenty-four hours of it. You will meet many different nurses, but they will each know all about taking care of you because that information is kept on your very own chart.

Nurses are handy to have around when you have questions.

Nurses work with doctors and follow their instructions. Nurses have assistants too. These helpers are called nurses' aides.

Other members of the hospital staff have the job of taking x-rays. We mentioned those before, remember?

There are lots of other very big and complicated ways to look inside you to get information that will help the doctors know more about you.

There are also clerks who write down information that's important for the doctors and nurses to know.

And let's not forget the person who puts together the medicine the doctor wants you to have. That person is called a pharmacist. Instead of working in the drugstore near your home, this pharmacist works in the hospital.

You will probably meet some people whose job it is to talk with you and your family to make sure things are running smoothly. There will even be a teacher who helps you to keep up to date with your work. And a playroom where you'll be able to find toys and games and other children to play with.

And let's not forget the doctors. That would be like talking about a baseball game and not mentioning the pitcher!

There are many different kinds of doctors in a hospital. There are doctors who only work to repair broken bones; they are called orthopedists. There are doctors who examine your blood; they are called hematologists. There are doctors who work with your x-rays; these are called radiologists. Then there are the surgeons who do the operations and the children's doctor – the pediatrician.

You may not be able to pronounce these difficult names but that's okay – some grownups can't say them properly either!

Saying them isn't important.

What is important is that when your pediatrician decides that you need to go to a hospital, it's because all the doctors with the fancy names will work together to help get you well.

That's a lot of people paying attention to one person: you!

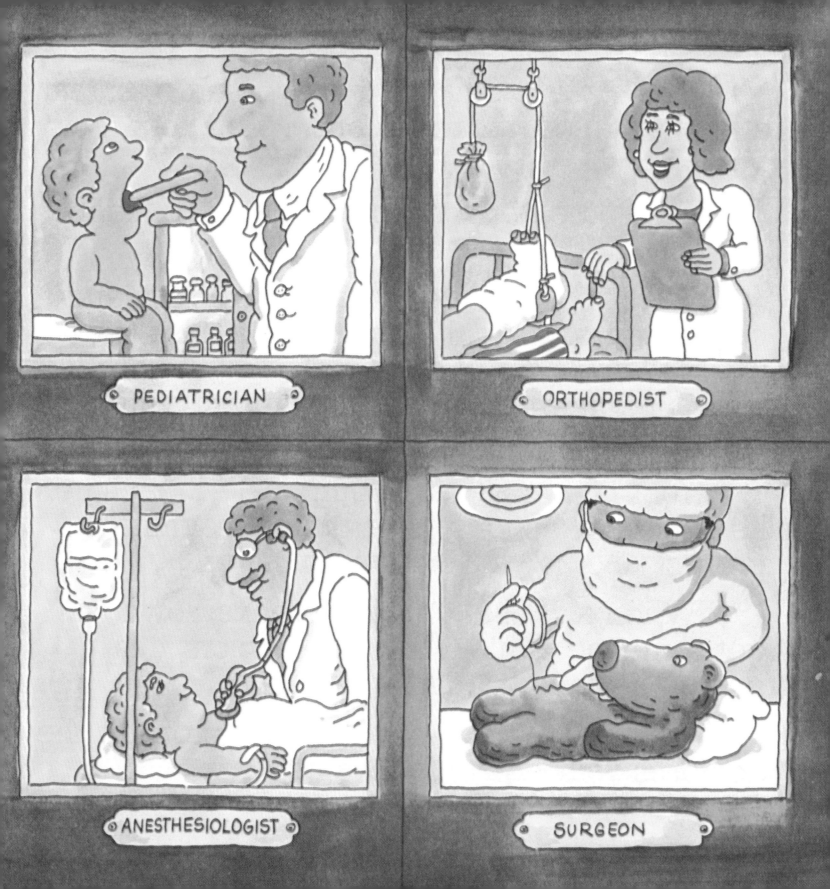

PEDIATRICIAN

ORTHOPEDIST

ANESTHESIOLOGIST

SURGEON

But you're special and you deserve all that attention! Since you're special, let's take a new look at you.

Did you ever wonder what you are made of? The stuff inside you?

Well, you're made of things like skin and bones and veins and blood and organs. (No, not the kind you hear played in church! Organs like lungs and heart and liver, that kind of stuff.) You also have lots of nerves and muscles.

Your body is a very complicated machine. It's built to last a long time. But no machine is perfect, and so your body isn't either.

When a TV set or a car breaks down we get someone to fix it. Like the doctors, this person has a fancy name: mechanic.

When your body doesn't work properly the doctor is your body's mechanic.

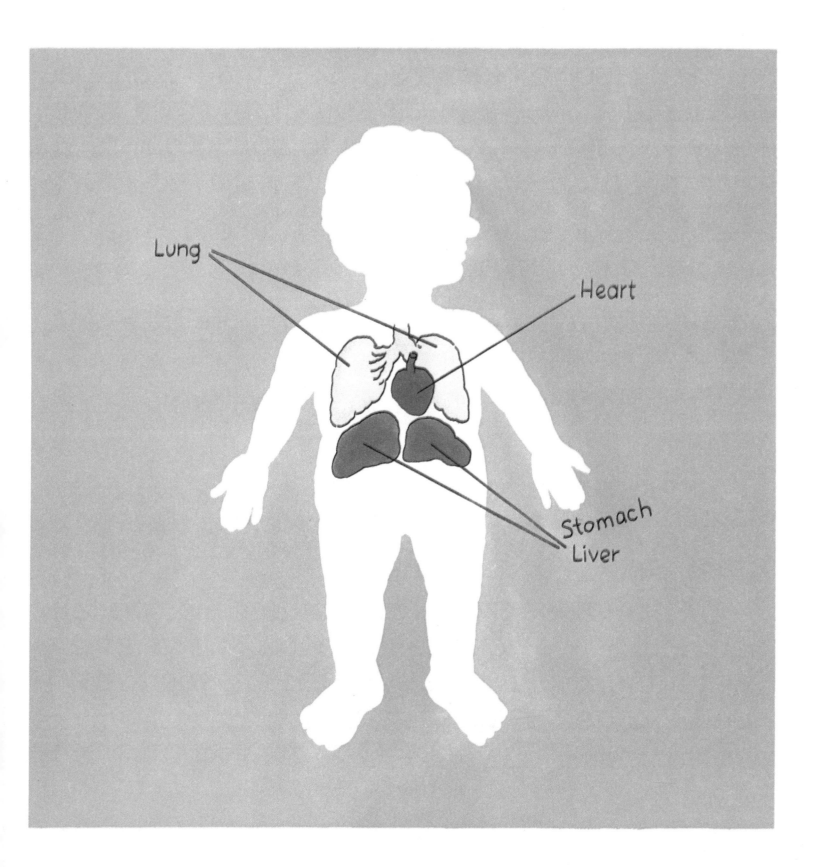

Lung

Heart

Stomach

Liver

Perhaps you found yourself in a hospital all of a sudden. No warning. You didn't even have a chance to pack your favorite comic books and your huggie bear. Maybe you had an accident.

An accident is when something happens to you without warning. For example:

maybe you slipped on a banana peel and fell down – hard!

maybe you fell from your bike, or skateboard. Crash!

maybe you were chasing a ball and forgot to look and something hit you – a car, for instance.

All of those things (and others that we left out) could give you broken bones. Or you may be hurting a lot inside even though you can't see damage on your outsides.

When any of these things happen you're brought to the hospital in a hurry. Sometimes even in an ambulance, or in a police car, with a siren howling and red lights flashing.

Kids who come to the hospital because of an accident usually are taken into the Emergency Room first. It's called Emergency Room because all the people who work there are ready to work real fast. Their job is to help people quickly.

The Emergency Room is a busy place. People are so busy there they may not have a chance to chat with you. Your mom and dad or friends may be asked to wait outside so they don't get in the way of the doctors and nurses who are trying to help you.

You might be hurting and maybe the things the doctors and nurses do to you hurt too. But that's only for a little while. Soon you'll feel better.

Remember, you're taken to the hospital because they have all those people and all those fancy machines that couldn't fit into your house, or even into your doctor's office. And they will all work together, the people and the machines, to help get you well.

To get well is the only reason you're there — not because you had a fight with your sister or brother or because you broke your grandma's lamp.

Unless you have an accident or suddenly get very very sick, you'll know ahead of time when you are going to the hospital. That way you can plan to bring along your favorite toys and books.

You can even bring some of your favorite food or juice. You see, the people who work in the hospital understand how you feel about being away from home.

If you can think of something else that might make you feel more at home (like leaving a light on at night), tell them about it. They'll do what they can to make you happy and comfortable.

When you first come to the hospital you are very busy. You meet so many people it'll be hard to remember them all even though they wear special badges to let you know who they are.

You get a bracelet with your name on it so everyone will know who <u>you</u> are too. And you get to wear it all the time.

All these hospital people get working to find out what's bothering your body. The nurse will ask you to pee into a little cup (that's easy for boys!) so they can test your urine.

You'll be surprised at how much the doctors can learn about you from that stuff. And if you think that's amazing, you should know how very much they can learn about you just from your blood.

That's why sometimes some one will come along to take some of your blood.

Blood? Yucch!

Yup, blood. But it's really important and that's the reason they do it.

Sometimes they stick your finger and other times they use a needle that goes into a vein in your arm. It may hurt for a second or two. Sometimes it doesn't hurt at all. And it is kind of interesting to watch your own blood go into a tube.

By the way, your body won't miss that blood one bit. Do you know why? It's because your body is such a great machine that it makes more blood right away and in a short time it'll all be replaced.

Many people give their blood—without even being sick—just so that hospitals and blood banks can keep it. That's just in case some kids or grownups need some extra blood in a hurry.

You might get a chance to visit other parts of the hospital when you have some of those tests we talked about. You get to travel everywhere by wheelchair with somebody pushing you. Pretty neat service.

When you stay in the hospital, it will be on a floor for children only. It's called the Pediatrics Ward but that's just a fancy name for Children's Floor.

There will be a bed just for you with your name tag on it. You'll see lots of other kids there. Some may have the same illness that you have. And some will have other things wrong with them.

You may see some unusual things – like kids with legs or arms in plaster casts, or maybe with strange tubes and machines all around them.

Some may look pretty sick. At first it may seem odd to see people pushing or pulling all kinds of gadgets, but after a while you get used to it.

Remember, this is a hospital. And the children are there because, just like you, they need special care.

Let's be honest about it. Being in a hospital may be an adventure but most children would rather be home.

Being in a hospital isn't a fun thing like being in a circus or a movie theater. You don't just get up one morning and say, "Hey Mom. Hey Dad. I feel like having some fun today. Let's take me to a hospital."

Nothing like that at all. In fact being in a hospital can churn up a lot of feelings.

Sometimes being there is scary.

Being there can also make you angry.

Sometimes you feel lonely.

And lots of times you may feel bored. Yes, it's <u>boring</u>!

But whether you are there to have an operation or just to let the doctors and nurses find out more about why you are sick, you can be sure that everyone is working as fast as they can to make you well so you can go home soon.

While you <u>are</u> there, you will meet children who may become new friends. Since they are in the hospital too, they know exactly how you feel – because they probably feel the same way.

Sometimes other kids can answer questions that puzzle you. Ask them. If they don't know the answers, ask the doctor. Ask the nurses.

If you think you'll be asleep the next time they come by, leave them a note. Doctors and nurses will be happy to answer your questions if they can.

Once you are cozy in your own hospital bed, you'll meet your own doctor and nurse. The nurse will even give you your own wash up kit that you can take home with you. Don't worry if you didn't bring your pajamas; the hospital has plenty that you can wear.

Here's more good news – you don't have to make your own bed, or clear away your dishes after meals. Hospital people do all these things for you.

Now just let's say you are in the hospital because you need an operation. Maybe your tonsils have to come out because the doctor has decided they need to be removed.

Here's what happens before the operation.

First you have to have a real empty stomach Why? Because the medicine they give you to make you sleep can work best if there's no food in your tummy. So, no eating for at least 12 hours. No midnight snack that night. Not even a sip of water! Even one nibble of a pretzel could complicate matters.

So now it's O-Day – The Day Of Your Operation.

Your nurse will wake you up very, very early. No sooner do you wake up than you'll probably have to take medicine to make you sleepy again!

The medicine may be put into you with a needle. Yucch!

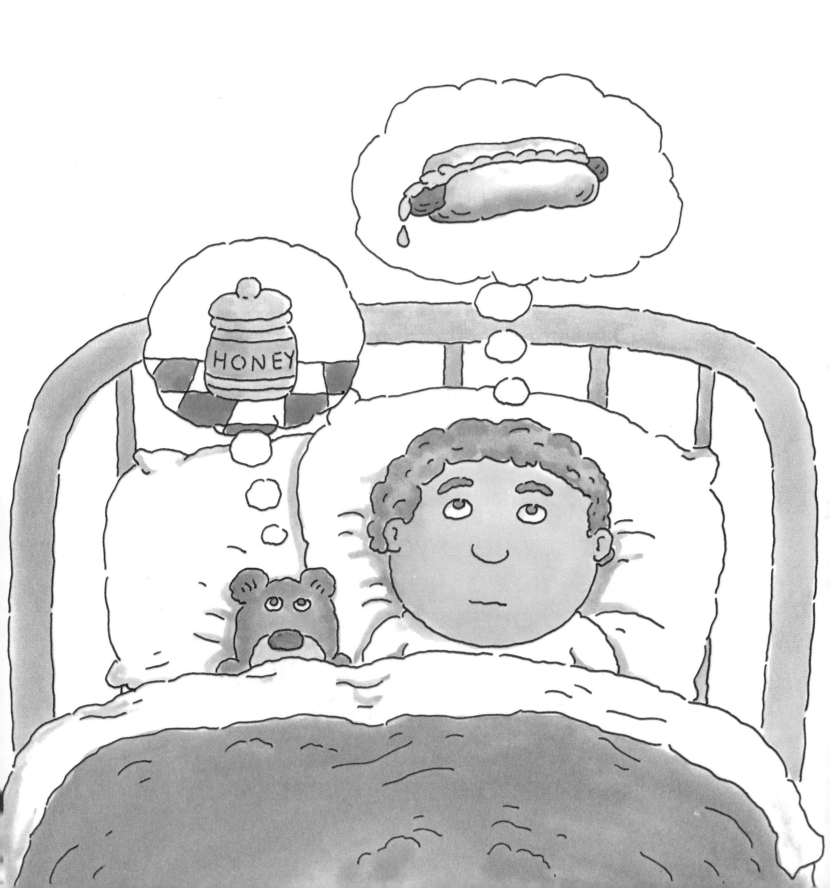

Next you are moved onto a stretcher. This is like a cot on wheels which you get to ride on as an aide (that's one of those helpers) takes you to the floor of the hospital where they do the operations. You'll know you're there because everything and everyone will be dressed in green or blue: caps, masks, gowns. But over those masks you'll see friendly, friendly eyes...

Doctors and nurses dress in this special clothing so that everything stays as clean as possible.

Your next move is from the stretcher to the operating table where you'll be covered by sheets. These match the color of the clothing the doctors and nurses wear.

Your heartbeat will be listened to all the time you're there and all kinds of machines will be attached to you.

You have just become a star!

You, a star in the Theater of Operations. (Yes, they even call it a "theater.")

You're a star but you're going to miss most of your own show. You're going to miss the rest of what's happening to you because you'll be fast asleep! It's a different kind of sleep than the kind you do every night. With this kind of sleep you don't feel anything and you won't wake up in the middle of the show!

The doctor who gives you the sleep medicine has a tough name to say: anesthesiologist. That's certainly a mouthful. (Pronounce it an-es-thee-zee-ol-o-gist. Not so tough, eh?) This doctor doesn't put you to sleep by singing a lullaby or by telling you bad jokes.

There are two different ways it can be done.

The first way is to put a mask on your face. It looks a lot like the kind astronauts wear. It fits just over your nose and mouth and it has two tubes attached to it.

You breathe in a special kind of gas that comes through the tubes and puts you to sleep. (Your dentist may have given you sweet gas to help when your teeth were being fixed. It's something like that, except you don't fall asleep in your dentist's office.)

Pleasant dreams!

The second way you might go to sleep is with the help of a special hollow (empty inside) needle. It's called an I.V. This is short for intravenous. This is put into your vein (it doesn't hurt once it's in) and there's a long plastic tube attached to a plastic bag. The doctor puts the sleep medicine into the tube and before you can count to "three" you'll be asleep.

A good thing about an I.V. is that you only need to get that one needle. When you need any other medicine the doctor and nurse can just put it in the I.V.

Back to the star – that's you!

By this time you are so fast asleep that the next thing you'll see is yourself – after it's all over!

You won't feel a thing!

When you wake up you'll usually be in a special room called the Recovery Room. Sometimes it's called the wake-up room because that's where you'll be when you wake up. It's also where the doctors and nurses can keep an eye on you after your operation.

Once the sleep medicine wears off you'll go back to your own room with your toys and books and new friends, and of course your family.

You probably won't feel real great right away. After all, this has been a busy day and your body needs time to feel good again.

One thing you'll look forward to is visiting time. That's when your family and friends can come to see you. Those who can't may send you "get well" cards.

Some hospitals even allow your parents to stay with you right through it all.

One thing you may have when you leave that you didn't have when you came to the hospital is a scar. Depending on where it is, you'll want to show it off.

Everyone knows what you want most of all. You want to go home. Only your doctor can decide when it's best to send you home.

Don't worry. You should be back on your bicycle before long.

Every child who goes to the hospital is there for a very special reason. <u>You</u> are there because your family loves you and wants you to get the best care possible to help you to get well.

If you have questions about how <u>you</u> got to the hospital ask your doctor and your family. They'll tell you as much as they can.

But before long, the best part of being in the hospital will happen – you'll be going home!